Animals in Danger

Janine Amos

W
FRANKLIN WATTS
LONDON•SYDNEY

This edition 2003

Franklin Watts
96 Leonard Street
London EC2A 4XD

Franklin Watts Australia
45-51 Huntley Street
Alexandria
NSW 2015

Copyright © 1992 Franklin Watts

Editor: Ambreen Husain
Design: Shaun Barlow
Artwork: David McAllister;
Martin Cosby
Picture research: Ambreen Husain
Educational advisor:
Joy Richardson

A CIP catalogue record for
this book is available from the
British Library

ISBN 0 7496 5058 3

Printed in Italy

Contents

What does endangered mean?

The dodo was a short fat bird the size of a large turkey. It had a curly tail and tiny wings. You will never see a live dodo. The very last one died over three hundred years ago. Dodos are **extinct**.

Today, many animals are in trouble. They are in danger of dying out for ever, just like the dodo. We call them endangered animals.

▷ The dodo could not fly. People and animals killed dodos for food until they became extinct.

Why are animals in danger?

Each separate type of animal is called a **species.** Hundreds of new species are discovered every year, but thousands of known and unknown species are in danger of extinction. Some are harmed by poisons from factories and farms. Some are hunted for their skins. Many species begin to die out when their homes, or **habitats**, are destroyed.

△ Fumes from cars and factories have poisoned the lake habitats of spotted salamanders.

△ The golden lion tamarin is quickly losing its forest home.

▷ There are five species of rhinoceros. All of them are in danger of extinction because of hunting.

▽ The land around this road was once a forest and a home for many animals.

Plants, animals, people

Plants, animals and people need each other in order to survive. They all depend on one another in the cycle of life.

People need certain animals for food and work. In turn, these animals need plants and other animals. Every time a species becomes extinct, part of this chain is broken. Other living things may be threatened, including people.

▽ Elephants are used to move logs in some parts of the world. They can work in places where machines cannot go.

◁ Bees help fruit and vegetables to grow by carrying pollen from plant to plant.

▽ People have been catching fish for food for thousands of years.

The changing landscape

More and more people are born every year. There is less living space for wildlife. Forests are being cleared to build cities, factories and roads. Huge wild areas are being turned into ranches and farms. All over the world, natural habitats are being harmed or destroyed. Hundreds of species can no longer find the food and shelter they need.

▷ Large areas of rainforest are cut down to clear the ground for cattle ranches.

△ The Queen Alexandra birdwing has lost most of its rainforest habitat.

▽ The Indian lion is an endangered species. Its forest habitat is being cut down for fuel and timber.

◁ The aye-aye is losing its forest home as more and more villages are built.

Newcomers

People can change natural habitats by moving new animals into an area. These 'newcomers' may kill the animals already there or eat their food. The newcomers may take over the habitat.

People themselves are a danger to animals. Tourists and holiday-makers can disturb wild animals and harm their habitats.

▽ Wild animals in their natural habitats are being disturbed by increasing numbers of tourists.

◁ People took wild dogs called dingoes to the island of Australia.

▷ Australia's own animals, such as wallabies, are hunted by the newcomers.

◁ The Mediterranean monk seal has nowhere to have its pups. The coastline has been taken over by people.

A dirty world

Factories, cities and traffic make the world dirty because they produce **waste.** This dirty waste is called **pollution.** Pollution from factories may drain into rivers. Sometimes fish are poisoned. Birds which eat the fish are poisoned too.

Crop spraying is another kind of pollution. Farmers spray crops to kill insect pests but harmless animals die too.

▷ American bald eagles are harmed by eating fish from polluted rivers.

△ Many Californian condors have died from eating poisoned animal bodies.

▷ Crop spraying helps farmers to grow more food.

▽ The Baiji river dolphins of China are dying out. Their habitat is polluted with factory waste.

Dangerous seas

People pollute the oceans too. They use them as giant rubbish dumps. Lost fishing nets and other floating waste make dangerous traps for animals. Poisons from factories drain into the water. Sea creatures become ill and die. Oil tanker accidents spill sticky black oil into the sea, harming many animals.

▷ Some poisonous crop sprays get into sea water and into the bodies of adelie penguins.

▷ Many turtles die by getting tangled up in floating plastic bags.

▷ These birds cannot fly. They are covered in oil from an oil spill.

Hunted!

People endanger animal species by hunting them. Some animals are hunted for their skins, which are made into clothes. Other animals are hunted for their horns and tusks. These are made into ornaments and jewellery. Some species are caught and sold as pets. They are transported to foreign countries. Many die on the way.

▷ Thousands of elephants are still being killed for their tusks.

▽ Cockatoos are taken from their forest homes, put in cages and sold as pets.

▽ Tigers are hunted for their stripy coats.

▽ Crocodile skins are made into shoes and handbags. Three species of crocodile are in danger of becoming extinct.

Hunting in the water

Animals of the rivers and seas are in danger from hunting, and from fishing too. People fish for food, but sometimes so many of one species are caught that it becomes endangered. Huge nets used for fishing can trap other water animals, such as dolphins, by accident.

▽ The walrus is hunted for its tusks. People use them as ornaments.

◁ Some species of dolphin are drowned in fishing nets used to catch tuna.

▷ River terrapins in South East Asia are endangered. People take away too many of their eggs to eat.

▷ Fishermen catch millions of sharks every year for food. Some species, like the hammerhead, may be in danger.

What can be done

Many species of animals will only survive if we protect them and their habitats. This work is called **conservation**. Conservation groups and charities in many countries are working to save endangered species. They are asking for laws to be made to protect endangered animals. They are trying to stop habitats being polluted and destroyed.

▷ Blue whales can now live safely. They are protected all over the world and it is against the law to kill them.

◁ The giant panda is the sign of the World Wide Fund for Nature. The Fund helps to save animals all over the world.

▷ The giant panda was once common in China. Now its habitat has to be protected.

Protected land

Many countries have set aside land as national parks or **nature reserves**. In these areas, wild animals and their habitats are protected. Nobody is allowed to build there and hunting is against the law. Park managers make sure the animals are safe. In some large reserves they ride in helicopters to count the animals from above.

▷ Komodo dragons are huge lizards. They are protected in a national park on Komodo island in Indonesia.

▷ Yellowstone Park in the United States protects animals like the grizzly bear.

▽ Buffaloes, zebras, elephants and giraffes live in the Serengeti National Park in Africa.

Zoos

Some endangered species are protected in zoos. Here scientists can study the animals and learn more about them. Zoo workers help some animals to breed. This is called **captive breeding**. Sometimes it is the only way to keep a species alive. One day it may be safe to move these animals to homes in the wild.

▽ Endangered snakes called Round Island boas have been taken to Jersey Wildlife Preservation Trust. They are breeding well there.

▷ The European bison is a species that has been kept alive by captive breeding.

◁ The Arabian oryx was bred in zoos in the United States. Some are now doing well in the wild.

▽ Gharials used to be common in India. Now their survival depends on captive breeding.

A last chance

Time is running out fast for many species. Not all animals breed well in zoos. Some species must be left in the wild in protected areas. Others, like the kakapo, have to be moved away from people. The kakapo is a shy parrot that lives on the ground. Scientists have moved some of the last kakapos to lonely islands near New Zealand. Here they are safe from rats, cats and people.

▷ Guards protect the last northern white rhinos in Africa.

▽ There are only about 50 kakapos left. Scientists hope they will breed on their safe island homes.

▷ Only a few tourists are allowed to visit mountain gorillas in Zaire in Africa.

Success stories

Endangered animals can be saved. Protection in reserves has saved the American bison from extinction. Laws to stop hunting have helped some species of seals and some tigers. The Nene goose of Hawaii was saved from extinction by captive breeding. Many have been taken home to Hawaii and live in protected areas.

▷ Thousands of American bison are living in reserves in the United States.

▷ The Nene goose is still breeding well at the Slimbridge Wildfowl Trust in England.

◁ The Juan Fernandez fur seal was hunted for its fur. Now it is a protected species.

Things to do

Everyone can help endangered animals. You can help by:

- Making a poster to try to persuade people not to buy ornaments made from the tusks and horns of animals. Put it in your window or in your classroom.

- Asking your family and friends to only buy "dolphin friendly" tuna. This is tuna caught without harming other sea creatures like dolphins.

Useful Addresses/Websites:

WWF UK
Weyside Park
Godalming
Surrey
GU7 1XR
www.wwf.org.uk

The Whale and Dolphin
Conservation Society
Brookfield House
38 St Paul Street
Chippenham
SN15 1LY
www.wdcs.org

Glossary

breed Reproduce. Animals of the same species breed to produce young of their species.

captive breeding Encouraging animals to breed in zoos and wildlife parks.

conservation The protection of plants and animals and their natural homes, and the care of the land.

pollution Spoiling the oceans, land and air by dumping waste and other harmful substances.

species A group of animals which can breed with each other.

waste Anything thrown away as rubbish because it is not needed or wanted.

extinct When every member of a type of animal or plant dies, it is said to be extinct. It is gone for ever.

habitats The natural homes of animals or plants.

nature reserves Areas of land set apart for the protection of wildlife and nature.

Index

Photographic credits: Heather
Angel 9; Ardea (C Haagner) 15,
(F Golier) 21, (S Meyers) 29;
Biotica (M Cardwardine) 13;
Bruce Coleman Ltd (M Boulton)
17, (H Reinhard) 18; Ecoscene 5;
Jersey Wildlife Preservation Trust
(Q Bloxham) 24; Nature
Photographers Ltd (A Cleave) 10;
Planet Earth Pictures (I Edmonds)
10, (J Scott) 23, 27.